THE GREAT GLOBAL CHECKOUT

THE GREAT GLOBAL CHECKOUT

MILLENNIALS, IGENS, AND THE GROWING EPIDEMIC OF DISENGAGEMENT

WITH
TODD CORLEY

The Great Global Check Out
Millennials, iGens and the Epidemic of Disengagement
by TAPO Institute with Todd Corley

Published in the United States of America

First edition, 2017

ISBN-13: 978-1548739133
ISBN-10: 1548739133

TAPO Institute
175 S. Third Street, Suite 200
Columbus, OH 43215

www.tapoinstitute.org

The TAPO Institute

dedicates this book to the

Millennials and iGens poised to inherit the earth...

and, the Alphas destined to succeed them

ACKNOWLEDGEMENTS

The TAPO Institute
extends its thanks and appreciation to those whose lives, work,
research, and support directly and indirectly contributed to
the writing of this book.

New York University
Jonathan Robinson

The National Society of High School Scholars
Claes Nobel
James Lewis
Danielle Bedasse
Susan Thurman

Villanova University
Bethany Adams
Patricia van Kleef

Executive Leadership Council
Ron Parker

Central Ohio Diversity Consortium
Tim Harman
Priscilla Hammond
Shayne Downton
Francisco-Xavier Gomez-Bellenge
David Sullivan

INROADS
Forest T. Harper

TABLE OF CONTENTS

FOREWORD

Much has been written about multiple generations at work: who they are, how they work, what they expect, and how they compare. In that sense, *The Great Global Check Out* is not unique. What does distinguish this book from all others, however, is the pointed emphasis on the youngest, but largest of the generational groups -- Millennials and iGens (formally, Generations Y and Z) -- and their emotional commitment to society-at-large and the workplace in particular...or, lack thereof.

There appears to be a growing tension, a boiling point if you will, of malcontent; one that has seemingly permeated every facet of contemporary life. From casual social discourse over immigration to full blown racial/ethnic clashes over divisive language; from violent protests in support of revisionist history to heated arguments against climate change: everyone everywhere has a gripe about something these days.

The rub is largely anchored in the accessibility of information, speed of technology, and requirement for more transparency and authenticity. Said another way: the generation of today can fact check you before you put a period at the end of your sentence; will challenge you with accurate information; and will gladly offer a rebuttal that will stop you in your tracks and reverse course. This newfound reality means that the use of alternative facts, belittling language, or biased assumptions will often cause today's youth to rally together and speak out in a chorus of opposition.

History will look back at this time of angst and unrest. The activities of today -- public and open public resistance to executive orders that impact women, 'dreamers', transgendered, immigrants, and the climate change -- will surely be compared and contrasted to that of the Vietnam era, in which protests were both common and controversial. Add the scope, scale and widespread use of social platforms, and the cry for more accountability for publicly traded companies as well as greater transparency of elected officials magnifies the fever pitch.

The unfortunate thing in the end, however, is that Millennials and iGens may already be CHECKED OUT...well before we can solicit their knowledge in solving the wicked problems that have arrested our country; well before we can enlist their help in paying our social debt in full; and well before we can move forward to a more perfect union.

Todd L. Corley
Chief Diversity & Inclusion Officer, OhioHealth
Founder, TAPO Institute

PREFACE

The Great Global Check Out serves as a wake-up call to leaders and organizations challenged with under-engaged employees. The book specifically addresses the growing cynicism amongst Generations Y and Z within the global labor force at large, and pessimism in American workplaces in particular. *Check Out* also serves as a practical guide; one that offers simple action steps to help captivate younger employees' hearts, minds, and attentions as well as aid in creating a more optimistic organizational culture.

There are six chapters dedicated to subject of employee engagement. Although each chapter discusses a different facet, all six approach the overall topic consistently:

- The overview highlights the current state of affairs; explaining the set of circumstances that exists within the domestic and/or international workforce.

- The history explores the known and assumed catalysts, causes, and drivers leading to the issue being presented.

- The prevailing issue is summarized into a problem statement, then formally hypothesized; comparatively and contrastingly weighed in test of disengagement's existing workplace impact and future labor force implications.

- Finally, leaders and organizations are challenged to seek resolves to highlighted issues. Primary chapters include a 'call to action'; easy to execute acts that we, The TAPO Institute, believe can help reduce employee disengagement, mitigate its contagion, and improve employer-employee relationships overall.

When reading *The Great Global Check Out,* expect to be taken on a journey. Chapter One introduces you, the reader, to Millennials and iGens (Generations Y and Z respectively). It gives you a profile as to who they are, what they are motivated by, and what they expect from today's workplace. The chapter also proposes (for the first time) the concept of pessimism and unpacks high-level trends on the subject as well as the business importance of covering it.

Chapter Two offers a snapshot of global generational "check out" via the exploration of Millennial and iGen sentiment. Here, the root cause(s) of cynicism, pessimism and disengagement are examined and its epidemic spread explored.

Chapter Three deep dives into the younger cohort's values, beliefs and views in comparison and contrast with those of their older predecessors. Historic and current considerations are taken into account for each generation and a modest tracking of how values have changed over time, amongst each collective, is drawn.

Chapter Four investigates how, why and to what level Millennials and iGens participate. This discovery surfaces through analyses of politics, social activism, technology, and the workplace.

Chapter Five covers the topic of engagement from not only a discretionary effort (or seeming lack thereof) perspective, but an emotional one. This chapter sheds light as to why engagement in the workplace is perceived as obligatory, bureaucratic, and one-sided.

Chapter Six features poignant research that corroborates *The Great Global Check Out's* thesis and full argument: that the epidemic of Millennial and iGen pessimism will continue to disrupt the global labor force if it is not addressed and remedied to a level of satisfaction acceptable to those positioned to inherit it.

Our intent in publishing *The Great Global Check Out* is to prompt dialogue and elevate awareness around under-engagement; to disrupt antiquated, 'business as usual' employee engagement practices that ignore the needs of the workforce of today and tomorrow; and to stress the importance of building a dynamic workforce rooted in optimism, hope, and acceptance.

EPIGRAPH

"In the 1950s kids lost their innocence.

They were liberated from their parents by well-paying jobs, cars, and lyrics in music that gave rise to a new term ---the generation gap.

In the 1960s, kids lost their authority.

It was a decade of protest---church, state, and parents were all called into question and found wanting. Their authority was rejected, yet nothing ever replaced it.

In the 1970s, kids lost their love.

It was the decade of me-ism dominated by hyphenated words beginning with self. Self-image, Self-esteem, Self-assertion....It made for a lonely world. Kids learned everything there was to know about sex and forgot everything there was to know about love, and no one had the nerve to tell them there was a difference.

In the 1980s, kids lost their hope.

Stripped of innocence, authority and love and plagued by the horror of a nuclear nightmare, large and growing numbers of this generation stopped believing in the future.

In the 1990s kids lost their power to reason.

Less and less were they taught the very basics of language, truth, and logic and they grew up with the irrationality of a postmodern world.

In the new millennium, kids woke up and found out that somewhere in the midst of all this change, they had lost their imagination. Violence and perversion entertained them till none could talk of killing innocents since none was innocent anymore."

Ravi Zacharias
Recapture the Wonder

CHAPTER I

INTRODUCTION

Today, Meet Tomorrow.

Millennials are the big players of the "it" crowd, with iGens following closely behind. In 2015, Millennials unseated Baby Boomers and Gen Xers to become the second largest living generation and the largest generation currently represented in the global workforce. Comprised of individuals between the ages of 22-38, the Millennial generation currently stands at a size of 75.4 million; while iGens, aged 20 and below, number 91 million.

Typically categorized as self-serving and demanding of instant gratification, Millennials are actually a much more nuanced group with attitudes that betray a new approach to solving the problems that come with adulthood. The slow growth of the post-recession economy has forced Millennials to re-contextualize their goals for success and to re-evaluate the "whats," "whys," and "hows" of building a sustainable life for themselves. They saw parents and grandparents lose life savings and homes to predatory financial practices and careless spending habits. They have watched terrorism and war erode economies, challenge governments, test the patience of world powers, and destroy remnants of hope and citizen optimism. They are witnessing the world around them transform through the rapid emergence of digital technologies. Having grown up with cell phones in hand, a lack of privacy is not only accepted, it is their norm. More intimately, they are experiencing anxiety over the far-reaching burdens of rising educational costs, a fickle job market, and cost-of-living increases at the outset and, for some, first half of their adult lives. Understandably, Millennials embrace a future in which transparency is taken for granted, pragmatism tempers their choices, equity overshadows equality, and social institutions provide the support and freedom necessary for them to achieve their goals.

iGens are quite similar to Millennials in several ways, but are certainly distinct enough to have developed their own identity as a generation. Like Millennials, they grew up in a post-9/11 environment and saw the impact the Great Recession had on older generations. Unlike many Millennials, however, iGens did not experience the unbridled sense of optimism and economic growth of America in the 1990s. Millennials played with legos, dolls, and pogs before graduating to portable screened devices as part of their daily entertainment regimen whereas iGens were all but born with iPads (rather than "silver spoons") in their mouths. Differences aside, iGens' transition into adulthood resembles that of Millennials. Those

3

that are currently pursuing higher education or entering the workforce face a student loan burden that threatens to undermine any advantage a degree confers as well as below historic average wages, despite a job market that has fully recovered from The Great Recession.

A key defining trait of both Millennials and iGens is their desire for self-actualization and their embrace of social media as a tool to achieve it. Both generations heavily rely upon social platforms to manage more of their lives and to express more of themselves each day. From news aggregation to fact checking; sharing advice to managing personal narratives; replacing credit cards and cash to minimizing the overabundance of apps and communication channels for the many organizations in which they care: Millennials and iGens love to share, value authenticity, and prefer to mass consume bite-sized nuggets of information. As a result, social content tends to be short, to the point, and transparent about its purpose; while social delivery platforms are used for immediacy and transparency, mandating speedy sharing of personal information, deleting of exchanged content, and restricting content size. In a world in which they do not yet have control of it or its systems, social media offers a space for Millennials and iGens to create, define, own and dominate on their own terms.

Pessimism? What Pessimism?

Take a quick glance at any of the top headlines circulating over the current news cycle. Better yet, take a look at the most recent feeds of Millennial and iGen-focused media platforms such as Mic, Vice, Vox or BuzzFeed. It should not surprise you to find that numerous stories, across all verticals, highlight a growing sense of cynicism amongst the two youngest generations. The captions alone betray a lack of satisfaction over the practices that determine the flow of social, political, and economic life in today's society – a society Millennials and iGens stand to inherit. And, if you look at the topics trending on social media, it is easy to find that same displeasure reflected in the content being shared. This cynicism, dissatisfaction and displeasure can be wholly described as 'pessimism'.

Typically thought of as merely 'a negative outlook', pessimism is actually a bias. According to Merriam-Webster, it is the "inclination to emphasize adverse aspects, conditions, possibilities or outcomes." Like all bias, pessimism is natural. However, research from Stanford University has proven that it can be particularly detrimental because the human brain rewires itself to be less and less optimistic with every instance of exposure to negativity. Without optimism as a stimulus, negativity becomes not only a 'default behavior', but a way of living.

These days, pessimism is a contagion; spreading from a few individuals to entire civilizations. In fact, developed countries such as the U.S. and the U.K. have a greater tendency than emerging countries to view particular trends pessimistically. For example, a 2013 Ipsos MORI survey found that 55 percent of Britons believed immigration to be a very big problem in the U.K. Likewise, a 2015 Heartland Monitor Poll revealed that only 29 percent of Americans were optimistic about leadership decisions within major corporations while only 19 percent of Americans were optimistic about the efficacy of federal government. These sentiments grew and ultimately lead to 2016's Brexit and the election of billionaire businessman and Washington, D.C. outsider, Donald Trump as U.S. president respectively.

While a somewhat negative view of various trends is common across generations and nations, why are Millennials and iGens particularly affected? They have proverbially seen more clouds and less silver linings. For them, moments of optimism are far and few between and any semblances of hope they did hold have largely faded. They have seen parents lose jobs and the unemployment rate skyrocket. They have experienced financial struggle and the sting of crippling debt. They've acclimated to a perpetual war against vaguely defined enemies and the threat of violence around every corner, both domestic and abroad. In other words, having grown up in wake of both September 11 and The Great Recession that adversely impacted 73 percent of Americans alone, Millennials and iGens have been directly and indirectly conditioned to expect the worst and view the world from an intrinsically pessimistic perspective. Author Denis Waitley says, "Expect the best, plan for the worst, and prepare to be surprised," and these are exactly the conditions that shape Millennial and iGen pessimism. Really, theirs is a coping mechanism, a type of pessimism known as 'defensive pessimism'.

According to Julie Norem, Professor of Psychology at Wellesley College, defensive pessimism is a strategy for managing the anxiety and difficulties that come with undertaking a task. The application of this strategy involves setting expectations low, carefully considering and preparing for any opportunities for failure or poor performance, and proactively pursuing a successful outcome in spite of any potential setbacks. Defensive pessimism does not replace optimism; rather, it anchors periodic, otherwise unchecked optimism to realistic expectations. Millennials and iGens are generally optimistic about *their* future prospects and *their* ability to achieve the various goals that define success for them. Yet, they are hyper aware of the possibility that any number of setbacks are likely to occur; especially when said critical success factors are defined by extrinsic, rather than intrinsic, sources. They have also come to anticipate a confrontation of the same difficult circumstances that impacted older generations after The Great Recession. As such, they have become resourceful in addressing their challenges as a result of subconsciously applying defensive pessimism towards meeting their goals. Millennials and iGens express this pessimism in their every decision; it is reflected in their socialization, purchasing behavior and consumption habits. And, it informs their work experiences and career choices.

Why Does It Matter?

Millennials and iGens are numerous (already outnumbering earlier generations), diverse, and engage with the world differently than antecedent generations. They possess massive purchasing power and stand to grow more powerful socially, politically, and economically. Their evolving needs and desires determine what is important over the next several decades, who can provide products and services to meet said needs, and how those products and services will be delivered. Understanding their history and values is critical to engaging with Millennials and iGens on their terms, especially for organizations intent on targeting them primarily.

It is important to fully grasp the permeation of pessimism. Millennials and iGens view life through a pessimistic lens because as the youngest and largest population segment they will continue to grow in power over the next several decades. They will increasingly purchase products, use services, create policies, and shift culture in ways that organizations must take notice and adhere. To service their evolving needs and desires -- and to ensure today's organizations remain relevant and sustainable -- the history and values of these two generations, and how their beliefs and experiences impact every decision they make, must be appropriately recognized and respected.

CHAPTER II

———————— **SENTIMENT** ————————

When it comes to traditional societal institutions, it seems like Millennials are consistently checked out across the board. They overwhelmingly avoid identifying as religious, eschew political engagement, hop from job to job (and are frequently disengaged while working), frown upon the burden of education as undermining its value, and are generally noncommittal towards making the big decisions that typically define adulthood (e.g. home ownership and marriage). Yet, at the same time, they present striking contradictions between their values and their attitudes towards these institutions. For example, only 41 percent believe that religion is important, but 51 percent have a strong sense of spirituality. Millennials are the most highly educated generation to-date, but are skeptical of the efficacy of the education system. Only 26 percent have confidence in public schools, and 38 percent are concerned about the high costs of education. Just 23 percent of Millennials between 18-31 are married, yet 70 percent want to get married. This paradoxical trend continues for government, healthcare, the financial industry, media, and other organizations, down the list.

This discrepancy between values and attitudes reveals an interesting fact that was true of earlier generations at the onset of their young adulthood as well: Millennials want to step out of the shadow of their generational predecessors and make their own mark on the world. They are ready for the world to progress and to embrace new paradigms of socializing, working, and participating as members of society; but, the world is still not quite ready to move on in concert with them. They do not feel supported, understood, or cared about, so they are apathetic in their engagement with traditional societal institutions. The oversaturation of generational check out exhibited by Millennials is, therefore, a manifestation of their struggle to achieve agency in the face of social structures that are outdated, inefficient, and ultimately ineffective at addressing life in a contemporary world.

iGens are slightly less divergent than their Millennial peers; largely because their coming of age has been in lock step with major societal shifts. For them, recurrent changes in overall policies, principles, and practices are the norm, rather than the exception. Whereas, Millennials have experienced the 'before and after' shifts, and hold on to memories of better times, iGens only recognize the latter and believe that today's realities are as good as it gets -- unless they themselves do something about it.

When Millennials distrust, devalue, or lose confidence in societal institutions, they either protest or disconnect altogether to force change. When iGens distrust, devalue, or lose confidence in the same, they disconnect as well. However, instead of mirroring Millennial disgruntlement, or waiting for society to change, iGens create their own utopian systems and customize them to suit their own needs and wants. In other words, discontented Millennials will 'rage against the machine' of traditional institutions and demand changes of their restrictions and confines. Discontented iGens will simply build a new machine.

Social Structure Shapes Our Lives

In his essay "What is Structuralism," sociologist W.G. Runciman asserts that social structure can be categorized as a "collection of recurring institutional patterns and the system of roles comprising them". Basically, the structure of society is framed by the major institutions that redefine and reinforce the inherent social contract between the individuals comprising that society. Members of a society implicitly agree on how they will each contribute to the maintenance of these institutions (i.e. what role they play), and generally (though certainly not always) operate in such a way as to support values that fulfill common ideals and result in the greatest collective satisfaction. As younger generations become integrated into the various structures and institutions that formally define society, they initially take over roles of lesser influence before assuming roles of greater responsibility and impact. As they take on roles of greater importance, they begin to redefine the rules of the social contract to reflect a more equitable arrangement that accommodates various generational differences in worldview.

These 'differences' occur because while values and attitudes tend to shift over time, the ideals behind them remain the same. For example, happiness is an ideal that members of all generations aspire. Yet, what comprises happiness varies from generation to generation, and how each generation approaches the pursuit of happiness differs based upon their particular experiences, goals, and needs.

The values and attitudes of generations typically tend to overlap somewhat, especially between people of different generations that are chronologically close in age. People living in the same cultural environment are (more or, less) all raised to view the same ideals as important. Yet, over time, they undergo advances in technology, are exposed to increased multiculturalism, global interconnectivity (as well as other factors), and take advantage of this forward progress to redefine the ways in which they chose to interact with each other and create things. Younger generations are still accumulating experiences and defining the goals that will ultimately determine their core values. While they may evolve in similar manner to other generations in their understanding of various social, economic, and cultural changes, they are also impacted by said factors in ways that cause their understanding to diverge significantly from the progenitors.

Snapshot of Check Out in Action

So, what does this mean in the context of our contemporary world? Simply put, traditional establishments are struggling to acclimate to the breadth and speed of the many social, economic, and cultural changes happening in modern society because those in charge are hesitant to change. The best practices of the past are often inadequate to meet the challenges of the present, but having optimized these practices over a long period of time, those in charge are hesitant to move away from them, even in the face of decline and inevitable extinction. Millennials and iGens -- who grew up with, and in many cases created, new tools for working, playing, consuming, and communicating -- are uniquely positioned to leverage those tools to bring transformational growth to the businesses, establishments and social institutions that define society.

They have already done this in many areas of their personal lives with success. For example, they may use their smart devices to quickly pay for goods and services with a tap or a mobile app (i.e. Venmo, PayPal) instead of carrying around a bulky traditional wallet. Millennials and iGens want to be free to optimize their performance of tasks with the most effective tools they have at hand, and be judged on their merit and performance, rather than the time they commit or any other non-performance based metrics. Yet, the members of older generations who hold the roles of greatest significance when it comes to defining societal institutions are painfully slow to accept these new values. They are resistant to Millennials and iGens and reluctant to integrate them, their knowledge, skillsets and abilities into their institutional engagements. Instead, the youngest generations are pushed to meet expectations set by members of older generations, compelled to conform to outmoded standards, forced to use practices that are viewed as cumbersome, and made resigned to operate with impractical tools in favor of more effective alternatives. Rather than accepting this way of working and living at face value, Millennials and iGens eschew traditional institutions to the extent that they can, and engage with them pessimistically whenever, however they must.

Evidence of Millennials' increasing disengagement with traditional institutions and values are readily apparent. For instance, Millennials want to structure their family lives around their experiences, preferences, and needs, yet they are still pressured to get married and start families earlier. Economic decline, stagnant wages, and changing gender roles have made it impractical to marry and start families during early adulthood; Millennials simply do not have the resources or financial stability to do so. Furthermore, the definition of family structure has grown dramatically broader since Baby Boomers entered adulthood. The "nuclear family" of a mother, father, and their children has given way to families of multiple shapes, sizes, and situations. Moreover, the necessity of marriage is no longer clear, given that opportunities to reap the benefits purportedly afforded by it now exist outside of it. Millennials have recontextualized marriage and overwhelmingly do not find it appealing at early stages in life.

Politically, Millennial and iGen voices are drowned out, and their positions superficially co-opted to earn their support for policies and politicians that are not truly representative of their interests. In the 2016 U.S. presidential race, Millennials and iGens were more closely aligned with liberal and progressive-leaning candidates, with 70 percent of those under 30 years of age supporting Bernie

Sanders in the primaries. Fifty-five percent supported Hillary Clinton in the general election with another 8 percent supporting third-party candidates (compared to just 3 percent in 2012). The fact that Donald Trump received the same 37 percent of the vote in 2016 as Mitt Romney did in 2012 reveals that young voters who formerly supported Barack Obama made a significant move away from the Democratic Party in 2016. Ultimately, however, older generations turned out in greater numbers for Donald Trump. Thus, delivering a sharp reality check to 67 percent of Millennials and iGens with a different vision for the future. Earlier in the year across the Atlantic, British Millennials and iGens received a similar reality check when the results of the EU referendum stood against their wishes. While 73 percent of voters ages 18-24 and 62 percent of those between 25-34 voted to remain in the EU, older voters not only turned out in greater numbers, but also voted to leave. Whether low turnout was the cause or the result of situations like these (for example only 43 percent of U.K. Millennials ages 18-24 and 54 percent between 25-34 participated in the 2015 general election, while about 50 percent of U.S. Millennials age 18-29 participated in the 2016 general election), the fact remains that large numbers of young adults are unmotivated to participate in the political process. Even when they do, it frequently disappoints (if not, betrays) them.

Education is another sore spot for Millennials and iGens. The cost of a typical college education in the U.S. is continually on the rise, as is the college debt load along with it. The average cost of tuition for private and public four-year institutions was $33,479 and $9,648 respectively for the 2016-2017 school year. Ten years prior those costs were $22,308 and $5,804 respectively. As of 2017, the U.S. student loan debt reached an unprecedented benchmark of $1.4 trillion. According to a Gallup analysis, 35 percent of Millennials carry outstanding student loan debt. Data from credit reporting service Experian revealed that Millennials hold the largest number of loans at an estimated 4.5 per person, while iGens have the highest number of loans currently in deferment at nearly 80 percent.

Many Millennials have struggled to justify the high costs of their education in the face of limited job opportunities and slowly-growing wages since the recession of the late 2000s. While higher levels of education are generally associated with higher levels of income, individuals with outstanding student debt are significantly more likely to have a lower net worth than those without debt. This harsh reality has even led some iGens to reconsider the need for a college degree altogether (although most still believe in the importance of education). Many are opting to pursue vocational education -- which tends to be less expensive -- while opening up to well-paying trade career paths. Others are deferring college for one to two years to earn and save money, in an effort to avoid saddling their futures with educational mortgages.

Check out is also a significant issue for Millennials in the workforce. In general, employees of all generations tend to report high levels of disengagement at work, but Millennials exhibit the highest levels. While they are passionate about career building and eager to make a meaningful impact at work, they are also passionate about their personal pursuits outside of the workplace and expect companies to address the inequities facing them and stunting their personal and professional development. According to studies by staffing agency Adecco, Millennials believe that the opportunity for growth is the most important consideration in a first job; an implicit acknowledgement that wages are unlikely to budge for entry-level positions. The promise of reasonable opportunities to learn relevant hard and soft skills, produce impactful work, and earn promotions is sufficient enough to draw them into the workplace. On the flip side, clashes in work culture can easily cause them to disengage or look for positions elsewhere. A Pew Research Center report found that only 21 percent of Millennials feel positively about high numbers of older workers in the workplace. Part of this may be due to their difficult experiences in finding good jobs, but can also be attributed to their contrasting work style and its disruption to the practices of older generations. As previously mentioned, Millennials want to work efficiently using the most effective tools and approaches. For them, outdated business software that de-emphasizes collaborative working is a chore to use in place of cloud-collaborative tools such as Slack and Google's G Suite; which streamline the overall working process and allow for real-time feedback. The hierarchical chain of command, layered bureaucracy, and office politics that are pervasive in the workplace are of no interest to them. Many Millennials envy the lifestyle of the digital nomad, and would prefer a flexible working arrangement that allowed them to choose when, where, and how they work. Unlike older generations that place a premium on spending time at work, Millennials prefer a result-oriented approach. Today's workplaces are improving in many measures that matter to Millennials, such as flexibility (two-thirds say that they have some type of flexible arrangement at work), but overall, the practices leave much to be desired, and continue to feed disengagement.

iGens have many values that align with older generations' sentiments about work; these include employer loyalty, face-to-face communication, and a strong work ethic. However, there remains enough stark differences with their antecedents' beliefs to birth discontentment amongst the collective. Like Millennials, iGens require opportunities for advancement, respectful work relationships, honest and transparent leadership, personalization at work, and instant feedback to be successful. When those things are absent, iGens check out emotionally, behaviorally, and ultimately, physically; resulting in high workplace turnover.

The pattern of Millennial and iGen discontent and disengagement continues across institution after institution. Many lack trust in the police, who deliberately or not, reinforce ethnic misconceptions and institutionalized discrimination. Many are increasingly skeptical of religious institutions, which demonstrate intolerance towards the LGBTQ community and lifestyle choices that are now common and culturally acceptable, such as cohabitation and extramarital parenting. They don't place great trust in the media, traditional or new, and are highly skeptical of financial institution; which were responsible for the financial downturn that negatively impacted their entry into adulthood and continues to stall their early adult launches. As consumers, Millennials and iGens are not interested in ownership and are increasingly bypassing traditional marketplaces, preferring to purchase and pay for goods and services digitally. They prefer the on-demand convenience and the low cost of web-based streaming platforms over traditional network or cable television, and the utility of Lyft and Zipcar over a variable interest car note.

All in all, Millennials and iGens want to engage meaningfully across societal institutions but are not willing to abandon their values to do so, and they should not have to. They embrace ways of working, living, trading, and communicating that are disruptive, but highly effective at addressing contemporary challenges. Many of their standards are different from those of earlier generations, but their ideals are the same. Therefore, the leaders of older generations must not shy away from change out of complacency, fear of exclusion, or failure. They need to trust Millennials and iGens to approach things in their own way, support them where necessary, and contextualize the societal merit of their work towards common goals. In doing so, older generations can earn their loyalty and eliminate some of the strongest reasons behind why Millennials and iGens are checking out.

Call to Action

To stay ahead of the generational shift in values, you must master the art of understanding the overriding sentiment of today's most influential generations. Here are two immediate tasks for building and sustaining relationships among them.

- Take concerns seriously. Consider conducting a listening tour within your organization. Holding a series of 60-90 minute in-person focus groups -- pairing leaders with small groups of cross-cultural, cross-functional, cross-level staff -- gives Millennials and iGens a platform to engage, share thoughts and opinions, and to voice their concerns. Use their feedback to create meaningful work strategies.

- Exercise more positive thinking; especially during difficult and challenging times. Possessing moderate to aggressive optimism helps build psychological endurance, resilience and safety in Millennials and iGens. Cultivating positivity will not only guard against the contagion of pessimism and dissatisfaction, but will open their minds and sensibilities (and yours as well) to opportunity -- both, key components for effective problem-solving.

CHAPTER III
VALUES

As Millennials and iGens assume an increasingly dominant role in society, the extent to which their values differ from earlier generations is increasingly apparent. Across the board, whether as consumers, workers, parents, or citizens, Millennials and iGens are faced with circumstances that have conditioned them to pursue goals that often sit in contrast to those of Generation X and the Baby Boomers that preceded them. From a sociological standpoint, the larger narrative of success as a frame of life in a modern globalized society remains intact. People still value wealth, status, family, and freedom in one form or another. Yet the worldview of Millennials and iGens ascribes to a new set of ideals in line with what *they* see as the markers of success in a post-Great Recession world. We previously discussed the pervasiveness of pessimism in contemporary life and explored the circumstances that have influenced Millennials and iGens towards viewing the world pessimistically. Now, we pivot to examine the values behind the differing viewpoints and goals.

The values held by Millennials and iGens inevitably differ from those of Boomers and Gen Xers. Primarily, because each generation's set of values was developed in response to the political, social, and economic climate of their formative years. According to the Pew Research Center, Baby Boomers were the first generation born after World War II (1946-1964) and grew into adulthood during the initial post-war economic boom. They witnessed the onset of the Cold War, the triumphs of the Civil Rights Movement, and the scientific advancements of the Space Race. Gen Xers (born between 1965-1980) sit somewhat awkwardly between the Boomers and Millennials and came of age during a period marked by political scandal (Watergate), energy concerns, the widespread opposition to the Vietnam War, and the normalization of the Cold War. Workplace, household, and cultural norms were also in flux. Millennials, born between 1981-1996, grew up in home environments that were significantly different than those of earlier generations, during a period of rapid technological advancement, greater personal freedom, and increased information sharing via digital media. iGens, born after 1994, grew up during a period of global economic downturn, and are digital natives who innately practice cross-cultural consumption.

Financial/Economic Values

Millennials began to enter young adulthood during the onset of the Great Recession, and their early exposure to economic turmoil and financial uncertainty forced them to abandon traditional career paths and redefine 'success' and the 'successful lifestyle'. The difficulty of landing a decent job after graduating college, coupled with the burden of repaying student loans, left them with less disposable income than previous generations, and forced them to rethink their purchasing habits. Because they realize that it is difficult to attain the assets of past generations, Millennials set goals that revolve around their core ethics and values instead of money and possessions; and prefer not to engage with organizations whose values do not align with their own. Their perception of consumerism has shifted from "new and expensive is best" to the view that sharing, frugality, and re-purposing are ideal. At the same time, growing up in an age where digital services have given them convenient, personalized, and immediate access to what they want has created an expectation of instant gratification with minimal investment.

Unlike older generations who favored home and vehicle ownership, living in sprawling suburban areas, and commuting to work and services, Millennials shun ownership, placing greater weight on city living and the ecosystem cities provide. They want quick and affordable access to work, goods, and services and an environment that affords them a high quality of life. They want the opportunity to easily pursue interests outside of the workplace, and they prefer the affordability of public transportation, buying produce at local farmer's markets, and patronizing locally-owned businesses. Only 15 percent of Millennials think that owning a car is extremely important, while 30 percent of those who own cars are reluctant about their purchase. In terms of housing, convenience and affordability are the overriding considerations and renting is preferred over home ownership. According to a 2016 Pew report, 32.1 percent of adults aged 18-34 are living with their parents. This living arrangement results from a number of factors, including a poor job market, stagnant wages, and rising housing costs. For those who do move out, career advancement and economic security are driving factors in their decisions. Low wages and the possibility of frequent relocations make ownership too stifling of an investment.

Having learned much from the financial tumult experienced by their debt-laden Millennial forerunners (and their economically jaded Gen X parents), iGens have become the most financially savvy generation to date. According to a national study by The Center for Generational Kinetics, 77 percent of iGens (ages 14-22) earn their own spending money, 21 percent had a savings account before the age of ten, and 12 percent already are investing for retirement. Strongly debt-averse, the youngest generation is taking a proactive approach to finance rather than a reactive one; choosing to ignore the temporary comforts immediate satisfaction brings in favor of long-term future fulfillment.

However, one of the most interesting solutions both Millennials and iGens have used to achieve the lifestyle they want is the sharing economy. The sharing economy affords them the convenience of building wealth and obtaining various other assets for a fraction of the cost of traditional ownership. Furthermore, if they do own an asset, sharing economy services give them the opportunity to earn money by allowing others to use that asset when it is otherwise not in use. According to a poll from David Binder Research, 74 percent of Millennials are favorable towards companies like Lyft, Uber and Airbnb. The success of Lyft and

Uber's on-demand rides and Airbnb's affordable and flexible apartments are great examples of businesses addressing the shift away from the constraints of ownership and the debt that often comes with it. Moreover, the emergence and success of the sharing economy affirms the shift in values beyond financial responsibility and frugality: it affirms that Millennials and iGens are aware of and turned off by hyper-consumerism. Instead, they prefer collaborative consumption, and choose to support businesses that cater to this model; abandoning the rest.

In her TED Talk, collaboration expert Rachel Botsman suggests that Millennials place a high value on community and that their definition of what a community is has shifted to incorporate the global interconnectivity provided by the Internet. Millennials and iGens have developed a natural affinity for sharing (even with people they have never met face-to-face) and it is second nature for them to apply their sharing habits to their economic decisions. The convergence of their community values -- along with their affinity for sharing, cautious spending habits, and desire to positively impact the world around them, have primed them to more readily open their wallets to businesses that practice economic sustainability in one form or another. Research from The Center for Generational Kinetics echoes Botsman's posits about shopping becoming a social, collective effort. Findings state that "78 percent of iGens used ratings and reviews to purchase a (recent) item" and that "48 percent...frequently ask the opinion of friends or family before making a purchase".

Regarding their attitudes towards brands, a survey conducted by Adroit Digital highlights some of the key concerns for

Millennials when making purchases. Price is the greatest concern; followed by recommendations from friends, brand reputation, and quality. iGens share those feelings, but in the end, prefer to save their money than spend it at all. However, when they do spend, it is largely earmarked for experiences over things. *Harvard Business Review* calls this movement the 'Experience Economy', which describes when "a company intentionally uses services as the stage, and goods as props, to engage individual customers in a way that creates a memorable event." This Experience Economy is evidenced by the growing fame and popularity of music concerts, lifestyle festivals, cultural experiences, fitness/wellness summits and charitable events like Coachella, Afropunk, Bhakti Fest, Wanderlust, Complexcon, Xanadu and Global Citizen in recent years. Various sources estimate that roughly 32 million people go to at least one U.S. festival every year. Of that number, nearly 50 percent (or, 14.7 million) comprise Millennials and iGens.

Work Values

Across the board, Millennial attitudes toward work are significantly different from those of earlier generations. For Boomers, success is a priority. A worker's value is greatly determined by the amount of time they put into working. Because Boomers tend to define themselves through their careers, work is extremely important to them. Respect in the workplace is earned by demonstrating a willingness to put work first, and authority figures earn legitimacy in Boomers' eyes through visibility at work and the breadth of their experience.

For Gen Xers, time is a priority. Where Boomers are driven to reach success by working long hours, Gen Xers seek to find a balance between time and output; working smarter, not necessarily longer (or harder). Work is a necessary evil for them; it is not always enjoyable but it allows them to finance their desired lifestyles. They are self-reliant and prefer to focus on efficiently accomplishing tasks as opposed to building relationships at work. They are also less deferential to authority figures than Boomers and value merit over seniority.

Millennials place a priority on individuality and personal growth in the workplace. They are ambitious and eager to take on challenges to prove their merit, yet they are also somewhat insecure and need a lot of guidance and mentorship from more experienced coworkers. Growing up as digital natives, Millennials are used to utilizing technology to accomplish a high volume of work within short time frames. Like Gen Xers, they prefer not to spend a great deal of time working for work's sake. They view work as a means to an end; certainly not an aspect of life that defines who they are. Millennials are skeptical and testing of authority figures, but highly respectful of those who can help them learn new skills, advance their careers, and move closer to their life goals. The ideal workplace for a Millennial places them into a flexible and collaborative work environment. It values creativity and diversity, provides plenty of opportunities for new skill and career development, and allows them to take on more responsibility and earn pay increases. As the most educated generation yet, Millennials value education highly and are eager to learn job-critical skills either through on-the-job-training or via continuing education. Growth is extremely important, as is job fulfillment - they want to feel like their work is meaningful.

Millennials also prioritize their career advancement over loyalty to any particular organization, and expect to hold several jobs over the course of their careers. They want job security but unlike Boomers, they do not expect that devoting themselves to an entire career -- working long hours at a singular organization -- will lead to regular raises in pay and increasing responsibility. They entered the job market at a time when well-paying full-time positions were difficult to come by and are used to taking on freelance work and to job hopping as their needs dictate.

Work/life management is another important consideration for Millennials. As we mentioned earlier, they prefer to work smartly and efficiently, putting in only as much time as is required to complete a task well. But their desire for individuality means that they expect to have a say over other working conditions as well. They want to spend less time actually at work, and more time pursuing personal development and community engagement. They also favor working for organizations that take deliberate steps to attract younger talent and make the work environment more convenient and work culture more comfortable. Responding to their desires has led businesses to increasingly relocate their offices closer to the urban centers where Millennials live, and to offer non-traditional job perks such as flexible working hours, unlimited personal days, onsite gyms or gym memberships, full-service cafeterias, and frequent team outings. Adding this kind of value to the workplace helps to satisfy

Millennials' desire to attain a high quality of life and allows it to retain Millennial employees for longer.

Although iGens are fairly new to the workforce (formally joining in 2015), they are not novices to the concept of work. Most of them (77 percent) have been earning their own spending money through paid chores, side gigs, freelance opportunities, and part-time employment since their early youth, and aim to continue doing so through their college years. This early exposure to work and to working has fostered a collective entrepreneurial mindset that appears to be guiding their existing occupational pursuits and will assuredly cultivate their career demands going forward. Given that the majority of iGens are currently under the age of 18, their emerging participation in the labor market is sure to have a significant impact on work dynamics for years to come.

When it comes to work values, early indicators reveal that iGens hold a different stance as to what is and is not needed to survive, thrive and attain success in the workplace. In its analysis of Generation Z, the Society for Human Resources Management found that the cohort is highly driven by money, job security, and opportunities for advancement and growth -- a marked departure from Millennials who tend to value purpose over pay. However, both generations do share in the dislike of antiquated performance review systems (i.e. annual work assessments and semi-annual development plans). Like their peers, iGens expect daily coaching, mentoring and advising; but prefer feedback to be instant, in-person, and two-way.

iGens -- 2.5 billion young adults occasionally referred to as the Boomerang or Throwback Generation -- tend to mirror the work values of their parents (Gen X) and work ethic of their grandparents (Boomers) in that they respectively favor of autonomy, independence and privacy as well as individual contribution, competition and facetime. Yet, despite all of their entrepreneurial fortitude, iGens are socially conscious and care deeply about their communities.

More than 33 percent of these 'philanthroteens' (as coined by author Beth Kanter) expect their employers to give back and pay it forward. According to the Winter/Spring 2015 issue of The Cassandra Report, nearly 50 percent of the iGens in the U.K. and the U.S. desire to volunteer in some capacity, 32 percent are charitable donors, and over 10 percent have expressed interest in social entrepreneurship. Accordingly, they believe social responsibility is not optional; they feel it is a mandate of not only organizations-at-large but, of the individuals that lead as well as those that work for them.

Social Values

Diversity and Identity

More so than earlier generations, Millennials and iGens value diversity and approach the issue with a spirit of inclusivity. Millennials are comprised of 44.2 percent non-white ethnicities, compared to 25 percent for Boomers and 38.5 percent for Gen Xers. The most ethnically and racially diverse generation in history, over 50 percent of iGens identify as mixed race or as part of an ethnic group. According to a Deloitte report, Millennials and iGens view diversity through a different lens than earlier generations. Traditionally, diversity is measured through evaluating demographics and attitudes toward inclusive practices like equal opportunity, integration, tolerance, and fairness. But, Millennials place a greater focus on respecting individual identities, experiences, opinions and ideas; iGens avoid categorizations and labels altogether. Furthermore, they collectively value inclusion and view teamwork, capability, and connectivity as critical to driving business impact at work.

Their greater diversity and merit-based outlook, along with their affinity for connecting with others and general distaste for traditional institutions and values, mean that among other things, both generations are more accepting of fluid lifestyles and supportive of gender equality.

Family

Family values have changed to reflect the growing miscellany and multitude of living arrangements, lifestyles, and work cultures that people subscribe to today. Regarding marriage, the majority of Boomers would historically elope in their early 20s and have children by 30. Over the past 40 years however, later generations have increasingly delayed these major life events until further into their adulthood. This behavior corresponds with the increasing entry of women into the workforce and the desire of younger generations to pursue career achievement or financial security over starting families. Additionally, the utility of marriage and the traditional nuclear family has declined as other values have superseded them in importance. Single parent families have become more common as divorce rates have grown, extramarital sex has become more acceptable, medical advances have created alternatives to natural conception, and flexible work arrangements have made supporting children on a single income a manageable possibility.

Furthermore, as members of the LGBTQ community gain wider social acceptance and take greater strides forward in civil rights, the acceptable view of family has expanded to embrace parenthood for same-sex couples. Family size has declined, from an average of four children per family in the 1970s to two children in 2014, and correlates with greater levels of education in women.

Through their increasing abandonment of traditional gender roles and relationship norms, Millennials and iGens are influencing changes in policies and upending practices that have governed the same; both in the workplace and at home.

Religion

In line with their general malaise towards traditional institutions, Millennials are decidedly less positive towards religion and religious institutions than earlier generations. According to a 2014 Pew Research Religious Landscape study, just 41 percent of Millennials believe that religion is important; only 27 percent attempt to participate in religious services on a weekly basis. Furthermore, one-in-four Millennials do not identify with a religious tradition at all. Despite their distaste for organized religion, large numbers of Millennials identify as spiritual in some regard. They have a strong moral compass, which guides their decisions, and give meaningful consideration to some of the issues that religion aims to address, such as the purpose of life. Interestingly, 52 percent believe in the existence of God, while 66 percent believe in heaven and 56 percent believe in hell. Yet, they are losing faith in the ability of religious organizations to have a positive impact on society. This lack of religious commitment contrasts with the attitudes of most Boomers and Gen Xers, who overwhelmingly value the role of organized religion in society, but aligns with Millennials' embrace of values such as individuality and self-actualization.

The underlying difference between Millennials and older generations is that they view religious organizations as divisive and somewhat culpable for the problems that concern them the most within contemporary society. Having grown up in home, work, and social settings which demonstrate far more variation than earlier generations, Millennials are more tolerant of non-traditional lifestyles. They embrace multiculturalism and gender equality, and believe that people and institutions should be judged on their merit. Because religious organizations tend to support conservative values, they often fall on the opposite side of the table on issues that matter to Millennials such as marriage, abortion, and homosexuality. Many also embrace doctrines that contradict Millennial values, and have been criticized for their tolerance of amoral actions (e.g. the sexual abuse scandals of the Catholic

Church) on the part of community members. So, while religious institutions stand as a rallying point and provide a strong sense of community and support for older generations, Millennials have chosen instead to engage organizations which demonstrate the ability and commitment to addressing the social issues that concern them without requiring their adherence to values they don't agree.

iGens' views align with Millennials in that religion and religious institutions, in their existing operational state, are ineffective at meeting their needs, connecting their faith/belief to reality, and engaging in authentic dialogue on their life issues and concerns. For example, both generations feel that the failure to use technology and to formally integrate social media into the overall religious experience limits religious bodies' reach and message distribution. Moreover, they collectively agree that participation and membership in religious institutions should not be constrained to a targeted audience, but to all; and that exclusions of any kind are counterintuitive to the tenets of religion and organized faith. Furthermore, iGens also parrot Millennials in terms of being spiritual, rather than religious.

However, said value alignment is not universal. The majority of Millennials have been found to be liberal in their principles; whereas, iGens are generally more conservative. In fact, multiple studies suggest that iGens – because of their fluid and trans lifestyles, behaviors, and beliefs -- will be the most agnostic generation in modern history; since, perhaps, The Middle Ages. Meaning, they are the least likely of all generations to actively participate in, formally engage with, or financially support traditional religious institutions; especially those unwilling to address their needs as they see them.

Fascinatingly, Millennial liberality and iGen conservatism is not native to religion; both blur into the political arena as well.

Political Values

In terms of political affiliation, Millennials reject being labeled as a member of any particular group. Yet, they are more liberal than earlier generations thanks to the influence of numerous social and economic factors on their adolescence and young adulthood. For them, the most important political issues are the ones that proverbially hit closest to home. Markedly diverse, the Millennial generation is largely comprised of racial and ethnic groups that have been marginalized and often found on the losing side of policies with long lasting ramifications on their forward progress. Additionally, young, white Millennials tend to side with the peers of color that comprise their cohort -- they lean towards the political left and support liberal approaches to issues that disproportionately impact people of color negatively, such as marijuana and immigration. Improving education and reducing the financial burden on students after graduation is a key concern for Millennials, as is reducing humanity's ecological footprint and advancing LGBTQ rights. They also want to address the failures of the job market and financial industry that they and their parents faced as a result of the Great Recession. They view government intervention positively, particularly regarding issues like income inequality, discrimination, and health care. Interestingly, at 17 percent of their cohort, Millennials have the largest group of politically disengaged members of the last four generations. This could mean that Millennials will become more engaged in the political process as they grow older, or it could signal that they doubt the efficacy of the political process in affecting meaningful change. In general, they seem to place more value on supporting businesses that address social concerns than on political engagement.

Political chatter abounds when the topic of iGens and voting arises. Rumor has it that iGens will transform politics as we have come to know it. Their care of societal concerns and conservatism around fiscal responsibility are just two of the many reasons cited for this supposed change. The rumors, though, may prove true. As reported in the study, "Generation Z Goes to College" by Corey Seemiller and Meghan Grace, iGens have scant confidence (and even less faith) in the current government. Grace and Seemiller reveal that iGens are genuinely frustrated by "the lack of progress", "constant gridlock", and ineffectiveness to address social concerns and to solve outstanding issues such as "education, employment and racial equality".

Rather than work to fix what is viewed as a stagnant and broken bureaucratic system, iGens prefer to create their own apolitical path via entrepreneurship. Grace and Seemiller assert that iGens intend to overcome society's ills using "good old-fashioned hard work", innovation and problem-solving.

Call to Action

It is not enough to acknowledge Millennial and iGen values, it is imperative that you actively demonstrate respect of them by practicing integrity and affirming positive relationships. The younger generation is highly intuitive and can quickly detect disingenuousness and inauthenticity. Here's a simple checklist you can use to earn Millennial and iGen trust:

- Take accountability and accept responsibility. Owning your mistakes and avoiding victim and blaming behaviors yields to a more authentic, transparent you and, allows them to better relate to you. By example, doing the same helps influence what type of leaders they should become.

- See things through to completion. There is nothing more frustrating to both Millennials and iGens than lip service. Consider setting short-, mid-, and long-term SMART goals, so that projects and initiatives make progress while helping you and them have a fulfilling sense of accomplishment.

- Honor your word and agreements. Broken promises not only create mistrust but, they can damage your credibility. Establish trusting relationships by eliminating hyperbole, by promising only what you are certain can be delivered, and by over-delivering on the expected results.

CHAPTER IV

—————— PARTICIPATION ——————

There is a growing gulf between older and younger generations as to how best to approach the consistently disruptive, livelihood-threatening crises that crop up these days...and for good reason. The common perception is that Millennials are disengaged and apathetic towards addressing major issues, but this is inaccurate. As previously shared, Millennials (and the iGeneration following them) feel very passionately about addressing the many problems facing society today. However, from their perspective, political action is an imperfect solution to an ever-evolving and complicated set of problems. While it is true that Millennials have a patchy record of political engagement to date, it is important to understand that they prefer to express themselves and advocate for positive change socially rather than politically. For them, political disengagement does not equate to civic disengagement. Instead, they believe that addressing issues via social channels is the most effective way to move the needle forward on progress.

Politics are Messy, Deceptive, and Exclusive

To better comprehend why younger generations are turned off to the political process, one must first consider how the turbulent political climate of their formative years impacted their perspective of politics for the worse. Most Millennials were still too young to participate in the 2000 election and had their initial experience with the political process between 2004 and 2016 (iGens similarly have been largely unable to impact the process through voting to-date, but have witnessed the same trends as Millennials over the past 16 years). The post-9/11 political climate is one of unabashed polarization, and the number of Americans who express exclusively liberal or conservative values has grown from 10 percent to 21 percent since 1994. Americans agree less and less on how to best address collective problems, and politicians on both sides have consistently chosen not to cooperate with each other instead of finding common ground. The September 11th attacks left the U.S. with a sense of vulnerability that it had never experienced before. It presented a threat that was addressed with hawkish foreign policies and domestic policies that encroached on civil liberties. The lack of political cooperation did not end with national security; solutions to economic and social issues that may otherwise have been addressed from a less partisan position became objectively wrong through their ascription to whichever party conceived them.

Millennials and iGens have observed partisan brinkmanship slowly erode the efficacy of political action in addressing issues, and were largely unable to do anything about it through their own participation. By the time either group was old enough to participate, the damage was already inflicted. U.S. political policies enacted since the early 2000s have had significant ramifications both domestically and internationally, and many of these ramifications disproportionately impact younger generations. Before they even had a political voice to use, it was drowned out by the people tasked with listening to them. Millennials and iGens became quite adept at watching the political infighting and listening to resulting gaslighting. And, while they waited on the sidelines, emerging technology began to develop a digital space in which they could share their opinions as to what they saw. While older generations have looked to politics as the primary arena through which to advocate for their personal values, Millennials and iGens found meaning and power in social networking platforms; which they could claim as uniquely theirs.

Counterproductive partisanship and gridlock are just parts of the reason why Millennials and iGens are skeptical of politics; another factor is trust. A 2016 survey conducted by EY and the Economic Innovation Group found that 72 percent of Millennials have very little to no trust in the government (79 percent of iGens echo Millennial sentiment). Lack of trust is a big issue with them, and while political corruption is certainly nothing new, it seems to have pervaded the political system to a degree unseen until the modern era. Older generations can point to the Watergate scandal as a high-profile example of corruption penetrating the highest levels of government. Other examples of high-level corruption are easily unearthed with a quick Google search such as the Keating Five scandal, The Iran-Contra affair, and Abscam. Yet, from 1989 until 2011, the federal conviction rate of public servants and elected officials for corruption-related charges actually decreased by 25 percent. Thus, the issue is really one of perception over proliferation, aided by changes in how fast and how frequently information is shared.

The media landscape has changed dramatically over the past forty years, and content production has increased alongside society's inflated capacity for consumption. The proliferation of television and cable/satellite networks allowed for the creation of dedicated news networks; and the digital revolution allowed news organizations to leverage new media and reach even larger audiences. Personal computers and smart devices have become commonplace, and the news cycle has shifted to a 24/7 schedule that necessitates continual updates of previously introduced stories to meet content needs. Millennials and iGens grew up in this world. One in which information is readily available and content is created and shared non-stop. In this world, political scandals both large and small are repeatedly covered and every detail is subject to high levels of scrutiny. Furthermore, the advent of social media allows for everyone to participate in this process; sharing their own opinions and analyses of a given situation to a potential audience of hundreds of millions.

Millennials watched the impeachment of President Bill Clinton play out and saw his reputation questioned as his deception came to light. They observed President Barack Obama attacked for and undermined because of his race, religion, and progressive stances on health care, the environment and gender equality. They saw a contentious presidential race leave many voters dissatisfied. Then, watched the newly-elected president and his cabinet manipulate the political process and use unreliable information to initiate hugely unpopular social wars with vague end goals. They saw politician after politician publicly stand passionately against corruption and misconduct, only to be later exposed as guilty of the very things they purportedly stood against. Eliot Spitzer. John Edwards. Anthony Weiner. Rod Blagojevich. Rick Perry. They watched the normalization of deceptive behavior lead to a political environment in which it is perfectly fine to cite subjective information as objective (or, alternative) fact and where elected officials can be purchased by those with the capital to advance their personal agendas. Millennials and iGens have been shown time and again (since their childhood) that political systems do poor jobs of serving their original purpose - which is to uphold the U.S. Constitution and execute its tenets of unity, justice, domestic tranquility, defense, promotion of the general welfare and liberty for all. They have also been shown that those who have roles in those systems tend to have non-altruistic motivations which drive their decisions.

If Millennials and iGens are not engaged politically, it is not for a lack of concern or motivation. They are not disconnected from or insulated against the consequences of the political decisions being made daily. They understand acutely that they will one day be held accountable for the outcomes regardless of culpability. They are politically disengaged because they believe that the system is dysfunctional, and the forces at play that desire to keep it that way are too great to overcome by "playing the game." (It is no wonder they shun office politics and workplace bureaucracy.) They are not satisfied with a system that prioritizes compliance and cooperation over collaboration. They want to play a role in making decisions, not just following them. Instead of devoting their effort to a system that they feel has disenfranchised them, Millennials and iGens are leveraging the power of social networking to supercharge civic engagement in the digital landscape.

Social Networking Levels the Playing Field

Millennials and iGens are often referred to as digital natives because of their affinity for technology and adroitness at leveraging technology to achieve their goals. They have been conditioned to view the Internet and services provided through it as tools for removing any and all barriers between them and their goals. Therefore, it should come as no surprise that Millennials and iGens see social networking as a viable means through which to affect real-world change. Social networking services leverage the interconnectivity of the Internet to bypass conventional methods of building communities. They connect individuals who share common interests, goals, and values, and are centered around fostering engagement on a massive scale. They provide a public forum in which all users have the opportunity to express their own opinions and influence the opinions and actions of others. Social networking speaks to the collaborative and consensus-building tendencies of post-Gen Xers. Research shows that 68 percent of the young cohort prefer to not to make major decisions without hearing the opinions

43

of those they trust, and 70 percent are more excited to do things when their friends agree with their choices. Social networking allows them to join ever broader networks of like-minded individuals who will not only affirm their perspective but also act passionately in service of it.

Millennials and iGens use social platforms to raise awareness for issues they believe are important and galvanize people into taking meaningful actions to address these issues. Through social platforms they can facilitate candid dialogue about politically unpopular issues that do not otherwise receive fair coverage. They can also coordinate widely dispersed grassroots campaigns into unified social movements that grab the attention of major media outlets and important public figures. Over the past few years, these tactics have been used successfully ad nauseum to bring attention to crises across a wide range of issues including civil rights, political disenfranchisement, economic upheaval, public health, and negative environmental impact.

In 2014, the 'ALS Ice Bucket Challenge' spread across social media networks like wildfire. Over 17 million people shared videos of the challenge, helping to drive awareness of ALS (amyotrophic lateral sclerosis or, Lou Gehrig's Disease) upwards and raising $115 million for research into a cure in just six short weeks. In 2011, protesters embroiled in the Arab Spring uprisings across the Middle East used Twitter to publicize the situation and elicit support from foreign nations. That same year, the Occupy Wall Street movement used social media to viralize their message and garner support from labor unions, politicians, and celebrities. The Black Lives Matter movement began simply with the spread of the hashtag #blacklivesmatter in response to the shooting of Trayvon Martin in 2012. It has since bloomed into a multi-city social protest movement aimed at compelling traditional institutions to acknowledge and address systemic discrimination against minority groups. The culmination of the fight between the Standing Rock Sioux and Energy Transfer Partners over the Dakota Access Pipeline in late 2016 saw the tribe's supporters use social media to virtually "check-in" en masse at Standing Rock. They also shared real-time footage and accurate information of the situation as it unfolded, exposing the unnecessarily harsh tactics employed by law enforcement officials to coerce protesters to end their efforts. When President Trump signed an executive order instituting a travel ban for citizens of seven predominantly Muslim countries in January of 2017, taxicab drivers in New York City protested by holding a temporary work-stoppage at JFK Airport. Ride-sharing company Uber lowered its prices and allowed its drivers to take on passengers in place of the taxicabs, a decision that came off as out of touch with the situation. Further hurting the company's position was the fact its then CEO, Travis Kalanick, was a member of President Trump's economic advisory council at the time. In response, users began spreading the hashtag #deleteuber and sharing screenshots of them uninstalling the application from their phones. Over 200,000 quit using the service, prompting the resignation of the company's CEO from President Trump's economic advisory council. Social media helped law enforcement officials identify and capture multiple attackers during the now infamous "Unite the Right" rally held during August 2017 in Charlottesville, VA. White nationalists and neo-Nazi sympathizers responsible for ramming a car into a crowd of counter-protesters that killed 32-year-old Heather Heyer and injured 19 others; for viciously attacking and hospitalizing 20-year-old counter-protester Deandre Harris; for firing a gun in the direction of other counter-protesters; and for countless other violent acts were unrelentingly "named and shamed" (as the media coins) with the assistance of Millennials and iGens. One sympathizer was even fired from his job when his participation in the violent event was exposed on Twitter.

Many of these movements did not immediately result in quantifiable positive outcomes, but the issues at their core were thrust into the public consciousness when they might have otherwise been overlooked or outright ignored. Movements such as these are incredibly influential and able to spread beyond their initial base of support to reach critical mass. They become highly visible and unavoidable, compelling policymakers to take notice, listen, acknowledge the situation, and address it by adopting changes to their platforms. To put it simply, Millennials and iGens leverage the massive social capital afforded to them by using social networks to coordinate social movements that indirectly raise their political capital. Social activism *is* political engagement.

Step One: Corporate Social Responsibility;
Step Two: Responsible Business Conduct

The same mechanics that fuel Millennials and iGens' social activism give them significant economic influence as well. In this climate, businesses are hard challenged to engage with the

46

youngest generational cohort. Businesses must demonstrate that organizational values are aligned with cohort values by wholly embracing social responsibility. The arguments in favor of adopting socially responsible practices were made long ago: consumers overwhelmingly favor organizations that have adopted business practices with positive social, economic, or political impact.

According to a 2015 survey conducted by Cone Communications and Ebiquity, 91 percent of consumers expect companies to address social issues, and 90 percent would switch brands to one that is associated with a cause. Furthermore, 61 percent use social media to talk about or participate in corporate social responsibility efforts; 34 percent would share positive information about an organization's efforts, while 25 percent would share negative information. Uber's recent misstep in the wake of President Trump's travel ban is a cautionary example to other businesses of just how tangible the effects of consumers' social networking activity can be. Not only did the company lose more than 200,000 customers; it also lost market share to its main competitor Lyft as customers spread a negative message about Uber's reaction to the ban. Conversely, Lyft released a statement condemning the ban, and pledged to donate $1 million to the ACLU over the next four years. Uber's actions, intentional or not, damaged the company's reputation and caused financial repercussions that could have been avoided if it had simply demonstrated that its values were aligned with those of its key stakeholders.

Businesses that intend to remain relevant in a Millennial/iGen-dominated world must prioritize the commitment to social responsibility. Yet, this commitment can be mutually beneficial. Millennials and iGens are highly motivated and already primed to make a positive impact with their actions; they prefer to support companies that use their resources to do the same. A business that incorporates practices which lead to positive social, economic, and environmental changes can empower those who do not believe in the efficacy of the political process, and who are maligned to political gameplay. Moreover, they can actively engage those who see opportunity to affect change via the exercise of their purchasing power and social influence. Prioritizing responsible practices can also have benefits beyond persuading Millennials and iGens to become loyal customers. Roel Nieuwenkamp of the Organization for Economic Co-operation and Development offers that responsible practices can mitigate financial liabilities, improve an organization's reputation, and increase its output. Operationally, this can attract promising new talent and lead to reduced costs.

Call to Action

Experts assert that the best way to gather the insight needed to inform your ideas, shape those environment around you, and inspire innovation is to observe, question, network, and connect with others who think, act, behave differently than you. But, the engagement process must first begin with an invitation to participate in open, honest, two-way communication. Here are a few other tips to spark participation:

- Call for a "questions-only" meeting. Instead of fielding answers to problems or mining for solutions, focus on generating thought-provoking questions -- one after the other -- to get to the root cause. One way to launch the interrogative process is to probe your team using the 5-Why Method.

- Take an object -- even at random -- and see how it connects to challenges your organization is facing and who you may need to work with to get a solution.

- Read and discuss news topics with your team to explore problems and challenges in the world. Together, brainstorm whatever comes to mind, examining how each could be resolved. During the course of exchange, observe how the team thinks during problem-solving, navigates decision-making, and encourages peer creativity.

CHAPTER V

—————— ENGAGEMENT ——————

For any organization to thrive it must have a clear understanding as to how to connect with its key stakeholders and motivate them to act in the organization's best interests. Goals, values, and core experiences vary across generational lines; which can cause undesirable friction between an organization and said stakeholders, particularly if they use incompatible approaches to engage with each other. Nowhere is this more evident than in the interactions between Millennials, iGens, and organizations today.

Millennials and iGens are becoming equally dominant generations within the workforce and the marketplace. However, in both arenas, they are highly disengaged when placed in situations that oblige them to operate outside of their specific viewpoint. To address this problem, traditional rules and historic tools of engagement must be updated to reflect Millennial/iGen lifestyles, communication styles, and working habits. The new paradigm must appeal to their worldview and demonstrate that organizational values align with theirs if they are to be encouraged to care.

What is Engagement Exactly?

Addressing the problems faced by organizations regarding engagement requires reflection on what the term means. At its most basic, "engagement" is the "process of cultivating attention or interest". To engage means to care about something; to care about something means to forge a connection with the object of that care. In other words, engagement is a relationship-building process in which a mutual exchange of empathy must occur and through which compassion is developed. Engagement is a two-way commitment. Parties must work to sympathize with and act beneficially on behalf of the other, in some fashion or another. As both parties mutually recognize the willingness of the other to take favorable action in their service, trust and loyalty are built; facilitating the strength of their connection.

There are many ways to consider the issue of engagement, but for our purposes here, we will examine the engagement of Millennials and iGens with organizations as workers as well as consumers. Millennials and iGens are tough cohorts to persuade as they are highly disengaged in both the workforce and the marketplace.

According to a report by Gallup, 71 percent of Millennials are disengaged from work, while 75 percent are disengaged as consumers. They present a challenge to the concept of engagement because their worldview and values consist heavily of egocentric attitudes. Yet, this does not mean that they cannot be engaged with or convinced to engage. Rather, when engaging them, it must first be clear as to *why* they ought to carry out mutually-beneficial actions; only then, by emphasizing the purpose, benefits and returns of such exchange, do they stand ready to receive in taking such action.

iGens are equally, if not more, challenging to engage. Because of the rises in global exclusion (xenophobia, racism, religion, gender equality, etc.), the normalization of alternate facts, and a worldwide crisis of trust, iGens are increasingly more trusting of their peers than of organizations and/or organizational leadership. This "trust deficit" (devised by Edelman Trust Barometer) can be largely considered as a catalyst for their increasing pursuit of entrepreneurship and their avoidance of traditional workplaces (non-startups) and traditional workplace roles (assistants, associates, managers, etc.). Distrust is also reflected in their consumer behavior. According to Interactions Marketing's "Next Generation of Retail" study, 81 percent of iGens do not have strong brand loyalty. However, like their Millennial peers, iGens can be engaged, but only under the right circumstances. Organizations that create a culture that embraces intrapreneurship -- one that is connected, collaborative, and creative; one in which highly driven, hyper-social iGens can embrace, grow and thrive – are the most appealing to this cohort. If organizations want iGens to emotionally connect and to fully engage, they must be willing to not only initiate contact but take (several) steps to ensure these younger voices, perspectives and opinions are included in every aspect of operations. Only then, can they earn iGens' trust. Organizations that take the risk in doing so find the effort worth the investment.

Both the facilitation of employee engagement and customer engagement rely heavily upon the process of building trust, and loyalty through an empathetic connection. However, each has different factors that must be considered if an organization is to successfully spur engagement amongst Millennials and iGens as members of either category. Chief on the list for employee engagement is providing meaning and balance. For customer engagement, quality, price, convenience, and conversation are key. For both, respect is paramount.

Employee Engagement

Although the financial crisis and recession of the late 2000s is firmly behind us on the calendar, the effects still linger for working Millennials. They still face a tough job market with fewer opportunities and lower pay than previous generations, and are pessimistic toward the process of career building because their path to a satisfying career looks quite different than it did for their parents and grandparents. Therefore, the way that they approach work and its place in their lives is also different. Job stability is important for Millennials who have financial obligations such as student loans to consider. In fact, research conducted by Adecco USA found that securing a job and repaying educational costs were the two most important concerns for Millennials in 2016. They are eager to establish their financial independence, so they are willing to accept the underpaying and unfulfilling jobs immediately available to them. Consequently, they are always on the lookout for better opportunities, and do not see a reason to be engaged in a position that is likely temporary - a stepping stone to better pay and better work conditions at another company.

When Millennials are disengaged at work, they display a major lack of discretionary effort. Discretionary effort is that which goes above and beyond the minimum level required in a given situation. For example, a member of the waitstaff at a restaurant must at minimum greet the customers who sit in their section, take and serve their orders, and deliver the check at the end of a meal. Yet, a waiter who is engaged will attend to these basic functions and be mindful of addressing additional small details that make the customer experience a positive one, without being coerced to do so. A more widely relatable example is an employee choosing to work extra hours to finish a project with a looming deadline, instead of just clocking out when the work day is over. An engaged employee exerting discretionary effort can have a significant positive impact on the achievement of business goals and objectives, and likewise a disengaged employee can have a damaging impact on a company's bottom line. Millennials can be very resourceful, diligent, and effective workers when engaged, so every effort ought to be made to increase their levels of engagement. Considering just their proclivity towards job hopping -- which according to Gallup costs the U.S. economy over $30 billion per year -- and their sheer numbers alone (they are currently the largest group within the workforce and will comprise nearly 50 percent of the workforce by 2020), a failure to address and reverse Millennial disengagement is an extremely expensive liability that organizations cannot afford to foster. Instead, they must revamp their organizational culture to provide the opportunities that Millennials are looking for, and encourage them to embrace sustained engagement within the workplace.

An effective strategy to combat Millennial disengagement in the workplace seeks to unburden them of the handicaps they have faced since entering the workforce and create an environment in which their strengths can be maximized and weaknesses minimized. Striking the right balance between base salary, advancement opportunities, non-monetary incentives, and impact (e.g. purposeful work) is essential. For example, providing reimbursement for educational costs and a reasonable performance-based raise or promotion schedule would offset the stigma of accepting a lower base salary. It would also ease Millennial job-seekers' concerns over reducing personal debt and achieving professional growth; minimizing the most compelling reasons they have to switch jobs. Additionally, bottling them into a system that obliges them to adopt a work style they do not connect with is counterproductive. Instead, organizations must allow them the space and opportunity to work in ways that come naturally to them. They need opportunities to work collaboratively and to contribute to solving problems. Rebuffing the top down approach, wherever possible, they seek the freedom to decide when and how they will complete tasks. Flexibility goes a long way towards improving their loyalty and productivity. Moreover, it improves Millennials' perception of their work situation on their personal well-being; another critical piece of the engagement puzzle. Research by Deloitte shows that 82 percent of Millennials with flexible working situations feel that their work arrangement has a positive impact on their well-being; while 81 percent feel a positive impact on their productivity. About 80 percent feel that a highly flexible work situation has a positive impact on their work/life balance as well as their engagement with work. Finally (but certainly not exhaustively), Millennial workers need encouragement, guidance, and support. Offering them workplace mentors who can guide their growth and coach their work performance demonstrates to them that the organization is concerned for their development. Thus, encouraging greater retention of Millennial employees.

In its 2014 Global Workforce Study, Towers Watson identifies three major factors that companies must develop to encourage sustainable engagement (or, the ability of workers to maintain their exertion of discretionary effort). These are traditional engagement (the willingness to exert discretionary effort), enablement (the provision of the tools, resources, and support necessary to do a good job), and energy (maintaining a work environment that supports the physical, interpersonal, and emotional well-being of employees). This lays out the true key to cracking Millennial disengagement in the workplace: an organization that cares about its employees and actively shows them will attract and retain employees that care about the organization and act for its benefit.

Although iGens haven't yet made a significant an imprint on the workplace as Millennials, their time is soon approaching. Just as transformation in the marketplace and the political landscape is expected, so too, are great changes coming to the workplace. If organizations are to build and maintain engaging work relationships with exceptionally driven, laser-focused Generation Z, their employer brand must be strong and compelling, their employment deal lucrative and competitive, and their work culture holacratic, autonomous, and innovative. In other words, to effectively win iGens' hearts and minds, they need competitive salary and benefit packages; true opportunities to grow, develop and advance; regular access to and conversation with internal thought leaders and senior organizational experts; and equal participation in and support of social activism.

Consumer Engagement

Expectedly, fostering consumer engagement amongst the Millennial generation requires a business to make many of the same considerations it would when addressing Millennial engagement in the workforce. After all, the same circumstances impacting their needs and expectations as workers are also shaping their needs and expectations as consumers. They are particularly concerned with price (low-paying jobs mean that every dollar counts), but are likewise willing to spend more on products and services they feel strongly about. They take the recommendations of their peers very seriously, and will avoid brands that do not have positive reputations. They also want flexibility when it comes to communicating with and purchasing from organizations. Ultimately, an organization must address both sides of the coin if it seeks to build strong reciprocal relationships with Millennials as they increasingly fill in the gaps left by older generations exiting the workforce and declining in collective purchasing power.

Millennials' influence as consumers should not be underestimated; research by Adroit Digital and Accenture shows that they are currently responsible for $600 billion in spending per year -- a number which is set to increase sharply to $1.4 trillion by 2020. This represents a staggering 30 percent of total annual retail sales in the U.S. alone. Yet, according to research by Gallup, as consumers, they have the lowest levels of engagement and the highest levels of active disengagement of any generation. Only 25 percent identify as fully engaged consumers, and across sectors, their active disengagement frequently exceeds their levels of engagement. In other words, Millennials have a lot of money to spend, but unless their loyalty is earned, they are not highly compelled to spend it consistently on one brand over another. Moreover, high levels of active disengagement mean that they openly express their discontent and seek to convince others to avoid products and services that they do not like. An organization that overlooks Millennial disengagement will find itself losing out on both potential profits and the opportunity to improve its reputation amongst a key demographic that only stands to grow in importance over time. At worst, it may suffer significant damage to its reputation, and incur financial losses as Millennials dissuade others from using a given brand.

To successfully engage Millennials as consumers, organizations must evolve from company-centric to experience-driven. Millennials are less concerned with how great a company is and more concerned with how that company and its products or services add value to their lives. Will it enable them to lead more interesting lives and strengthen their personal brands? Can they create a unique and memorable story around a product or service? Does a product or service empower them to address a social cause they feel passionately about? They must be able to convincingly answer 'yes' to each of these questions in order to feel engaged. Additionally, just as Millennials desire to be collaborators and co-creators in the workplace, they desire to collaborate with companies in creating and representing a brand's identity to their peers. They love being influencers; so, naturally, social media channels provide ideal forums for them to do so. They write product and service reviews, like and share the Facebook pages of organizations they connect with, and participate in hashtag campaigns that link brands to their personal stories via photos, short video clips, and other personalized media. Many also create video blogs discussing products and services in depth and encourage their digital communities to either use or avoid those products.

Convenience is a necessity. As digital natives, Millennials are accustomed to the convenience and immediacy provided by the internet and want a seamless transition between their interactions with companies digitally and in real life. The same personalized and supportive experience they find when browsing a company's retail website is the same experience they expect when they enter a brick-and-mortar shop, and they expect this to be facilitated through their mobile devices. Finally, in terms of communicating, Millennials want to be personally addressed and included in messaging across all touch points. According to research by Adroit Digital, 38 percent of Millennials want to see brands become more focused on them as consumers, while 52 percent prefer to engage with brands that are open to change based on their opinions and feedback. Brands must be transparent and conversations must be two-way interactions, or risk coming off as inauthentic. Furthermore, Millennials don't want to simply fall in line or be told what to do. They value making informed decisions based upon reliable information. Because of this, they are more likely to engage with and recommend brands that focus on quality, truthful messaging, and courting them as valued customers.

Sprite's "Wanna Sprite" campaign is a great example of a brand approaching Millennial consumers with engagement in mind. It works because, on every level, it acknowledges that the audience is ultimately in control of whether or not they choose to drink Sprite, but parodies the typical use of various marketing tactics to convince consumers to purchase a product. Moreover, the inclusion of the hashtag #wannasprite cleverly subverts Millennials' desire for brands to focus on them by incorporating the brand into the consumer's desire to have a drink. The hashtag also serves as an invitation for consumers to take control of the brand's narrative across various social media channels and make it their own.

As shared earlier, iGens are gamechangers politically and socially; the same holds true for them economically. Possessing a current buying power of $44 billion, it is reported that 93 percent of them already have influence over the purchase perceptions and behaviors of their families. However, Generation Z -- which will account for 40 percent of all consumers by 2020 -- is considered the least trusting of brands than any other generation; a fact that proves especially challenging for businesses. CEO of digital media company Dose, Emerson Spartz explains, "They (iGens) have the strongest BS filter because they've grown up in an era where information was available at all times."

In the past, brands were able to solidify their place in the home by creating campaigns that appealed to various members of the family. These days, if brands wish to reach families, they have to first pass muster with the iGen at home. To do so, businesses must be transparent about their product offerings, their products' ingredients (from ingredient integrity, i.e. organic or not, to sourcing origin, i.e. farmed raised or wild caught), and those who make/ship/distribute said products. Likewise, businesses must offer products that 'do no harm' (to the environment or human ecosystem) and be willing to contribute to the greatest good (charitably, socially). Finally, businesses must employ and be adept at using technology and social media to communicate and build relationships with iGens and their peer communities. Influencer marketing agency MediaKix reports 85 percent of iGens learn about new products through social media, 83 percent trust product information shared by other shoppers on social media more than advertising; 69 percent visit a store based on a retailer's social media post; 63 percent prefer to see social media influencers in product promotions; and nearly 50 percent connect online -- simultaneously across five screens (smartphones, TVs, laptops, desktops, and tablets) for an average 10 hours per day. Businesses and (future) employers will fail to connect, let alone engage with iGens, if they are not careful to take concerted note of their demands.

Millennials and iGens are shrewd consumers and ambitious workers, but are frequently disengaged when presented with conditions that fail to capture their concern. Yet, they are passionate, loyal, and highly effective when properly motivated. Organizations that understand and embrace their worldview stand to reap considerable benefits by adopting new practices which mitigate disengagement and allow Millennials and iGens to thrive.

Call to Action

Successfully engaging today's younger generations at work means isolating what motivates *them*. Remember, none are right or wrong. Give Millennials and iGens a platform to share of themselves and you'll find they'll open the door for you to do the same. Here are some ideas:

- Engage in design thinking. Work together to create something that people (team members, customers, etc.) will love.

- Actively practice inclusion. Think of who on your team is an untapped natural resource and call on them to help hack your organization's next big problem.

- Partner together on philanthropic projects. Show the world you and your team can help others.

CHAPTER VI

—————— EPIDEMIC ——————

While most of the trends explored in this book largely reflect the generational attitudes, sentiments, and behaviors of American Millennials and iGens; these beliefs are mirrored uniformly worldwide. That is to say, Generations Y and Z of all cultures, economies, and quality of life are touched by pessimism. Evidence of this is revealed in Aon's 2017 Trends in Global Employee Engagement Report. The report indicates that for the first since 2012, global engagement has regressed. It goes on to reveal that "growing cynicism about the workplace" as well as "increasing ambiguity about the future" have become contributing factors of "absenteeism, poor performance, workplace safety issues, and even cyber security breaches". The following highlights echo these trends.

Voice and Views

The World Economic Forum surveyed nearly 25,000 people between the ages of 18 and 35, from 186 countries and territories, for its Global Shapers Annual Survey 2017. It found that 56 percent of Millennial and iGen respondents felt that they were "not being listened to by global decision makers" and that their "views are not being taken into account before important decisions are made". These opinions are especially true of topic of climate change. Over 90 percent of Millennials and iGens "agree or strongly agree that humans are responsible for climate change" and nearly 49 percent believe that "destruction of nature" is the world's most serious global issue. In fact, when U.S. President Trump (staunch denier of global warming) withdrew American support of the over 100 country Paris Climate Accord in June of 2017, the world united in protest.

Leadership

The results of the Global Shapers Annual Survey 2017 echo the Edelman Trust Barometer data in that Millennials and iGens worldwide are deeply distrustful of large companies, banks, governments, and the media. Although they believe the three "most important characteristics of country leaders" are "integrity, honesty and humility" (47 percent), being "action-oriented" (34 percent), and having a willingness to "protect future of country" (30 percent), they also worry about the pervasiveness of widespread corruption (23 percent). Despite the latter, *Harvard Business Review* reports that leadership itself and taking on the role of leader was still considered "important" (61 percent Gen Y and Z, respectively).

Self-Identity

Like their American peers, global Millennials and iGens principally reject societal labels; preferring to self-identify as human first (41 percent) and global citizen second (19 percent). Collectively, they believe that all citizens deserve equal access of opportunities (51 percent), the ability to live without fear (32 percent) and the ability to work and live anywhere (25 percent). Actually, over 78 percent of them would welcome refugees in their own neighborhood. Yet, from Syria to the U.S., large scale conflicts and wars continue to be waged over supremacism, ethnocentrism, equality, and immigration.

Technology

Nearly 80 percent of global Millennials and iGens believe technology creates more jobs, rather than destroys them. However, a study from Universum, INSEAD Emerging Markets Institute, The HEAD Foundation and MIT Leadership Center unveiled that the cohort has an unfavorable view of organizations' digital capabilities to meet or match future demands of the workforce (particularly as it relates to flexibility, online training and development, international job exchanges and the like). As detailed in Aon's 2017 Trends in Global Employee Engagement Report, disruptive technologies are "challenging organizations in an unprecedented way." Although the challenge here is just as much a leadership issue as it is a systems infrastructure issue. Without the marriage of innovative leadership, healthy capital investments in technology, a competitive employee value proposition, and a clear strategy for the future, Millennials and iGens will continue to grow pessimistic, will check out of their workplaces and will divorce themselves from the traditional workplace altogether. For these cohorts, education, healthcare, and manufacturing – the industries with the greatest impact on quality of life -- are the top three sectors they feel could most benefit from technology disruption.

Entrepreneurship

Although the concepts of capitalism and entrepreneurship are steeped in American tradition, they are not indigenous to the West alone. In fact, the previously mentioned Universum/INSEAD/HEAD/MIT study revealed that Millennials and iGens in countries such as Mexico (57 percent), the UAE (56 percent), and India (43 percent) are most eager to start their own businesses and would prefer to do so over building a traditional career; even one with an international company. With global entrepreneurship at an all-time high, the populations of Japan and Australia (amongst other countries) rapidly aging, and the workforce of the European Union and U.S. shrinking (U.S. Boomers currently retire at a rate of 10,000 per day), the global labor force could experience a talent drought of engaged workers like never before.

FINAL THOUGHT

Although the picture painted throughout this discourse may seem terrifying at most, dismal at best, we at The TAPO Institute see an opportunity for you, our reader, as well as your organization(s) and leaders alike.

Consider, in a few short years (2025 to be exact), Millennials and iGens will comprise a nearly 80 percent of the global workforce; making it the largest, most diverse, savviest, educated, entrepreneurial, nimble and agile generations in history. Picture having that cache of talent -- that endless source of innovation, creativity, and competitiveness -- working for, with, and/or within your institution(s).

Imagine architecting the ideal inclusive organizational culture that nurtures an optimistic employee engagement experience. One in which technology is celebrated; social values and beliefs are equally respected; voices, views and opinions are solicited and cultivated; organizational fit is defined by performance, rather than bias and preference; and diversity is the norm, not the exception.

Now, visualize getting out of your own way to create opportunities that will heal the workforce of today (Millennials/Generation Y), help the workforce of tomorrow (iGens/Generation Z) and save the workforce of the future (Alphas/Generation A).

AFTERWORD

"If future generations are to remember us more with gratitude than sorrow, we must achieve more than just the miracles of technology. We must also leave them a glimpse of the world as it was created, not just as it looked when we got through with it."

Lyndon B. Johnson

REFERENCES

Overview References

Abramovich, G. (2015). 15 mind-blowing stats about generation Z. Retrieved from http://www.cmo.com/features/articles/2015/6/11/15-mind-blowing-stats-about-generation-z.html

Abramovich, G. (2017). Study: Majority of people more loyal to brands that care about them. Retrieved from http://www.cmo.com/features/articles/2017/1/23/wunderman-tlp-wantedness-study.html

Beall, G. (2016). 8 key differences between gen Z and millennials. Retrieved from http://www.huffingtonpost.com/george-beall/8-key-differences-between_b_12814200.html

Brownstein, R. (2015). America's growing pessimism. The Atlantic. Retrieved from https://www.theatlantic.com/politics/archive/2015/10/americans-pessimism-future/409564/

Defensive pessimism | applied social psychology (ASP). (2014). Retrieved from https://sites.psu.edu/aspsy/2014/04/08/defensive-pessimism/

Definition of PESSIMISM. Retrieved from https://www.merriam-webster.com/dictionary/pessimism

The deloitte millennial survey 2017 - apprehensive millennials: Seeking stability and opportunities in an uncertain world. (2017). Deloitte.

A divided and pessimistic electorate. (2016). Retrieved from http://www.people-press.org/2016/11/10/a-divided-and-pessimistic-electorate/

Finch, J. (2015). What is generation Z, and what does it want? Retrieved from https://www.fastcompany.com/3045317/what-is-generation-z-and-what-does-it-want

Fry, R. (2016). Millennials overtake baby boomers as america's largest generation. Retrieved from http://www.pewresearch.org/fact-tank/2016/04/25/millennials-overtake-baby-boomers/

Gen Z 2025: The final generation. (2015). Sparks & Honey. Retrieved from https://www.slideshare.net/sparksandhoney/gen-z-2025-the-final-generation-preview/29-
GEN Z 2025download Gen Z

Keller, A. C., Samuel, R., Bergman, M. M., & Semmer, N. K. (2014). Psychological, educational, and sociological perspectives on success and well-being in career development Springer.

Khazan, O. (2014). The upside of pessimism. The Atlantic. Retrieved from https://www.theatlantic.com/health/archive/2014/09/dont-think-positively/379993/

McMullen, T. Millennials pessimism could spell trouble for the U.S. housing market. Retrieved from http://www.forbes.com/sites/troymcmullen/2016/08/26/millennials-pessimism-could-spell-trouble-for-the-housing-market-in-the-u-s/

Meet generation Z: Forget everything you learned about millennials (2014). Sparks & Honey.

Millennials panel discussion | world built environment forum 2016. [Video/DVD] https://www.youtube.com/watch?v=42sP3hPzXQo

Nagdy, M., & Roser, M. (2016). Optimism & pessimism. Retrieved from https://ourworldindata.org/optimism-pessimism/

Oster, E. (2014). This gen Z infographic can help marketers get wise to the future. Retrieved from http://www.adweek.com/brand-marketing/gen-z-infographic-can-help-marketers-get-wise-future-159642/

Perils of perception survey. (2016). Ipsos MORI.

Schawbel, D. (2014). Gen Z employees: The 5 attributes you need to know. Retrieved from https://www.entrepreneur.com/article/236560

Team CGK (2015). Five generations of employees in today's workforce. Retrieved from http://genhq.com/five-generations-of-employees-in-todays-workforce/

United states census bureau statistics. (2017). Retrieved from https://www.census.gov/popclock/

Way to work survey results | adecco USA. (2015). Adecco Staffing. Retrieved from http://blog.adeccousa.com/way-to-work-survey-1/

Participation References

The ALS association ice bucket challenge FAQ. Retrieved from http://www.alsa.org/about-us/ice-bucket-challenge-faq.html

Amnesty International. The 'arab spring': Five years on. Retrieved from https://www.amnesty.org/en/latest/campaigns/2016/01/arab-spring-five-years-on/

Blake, A. (2017). Trump's travel ban is the controversial policy almost nobody was begging for. Washington Post. Retrieved from https://www.washingtonpost.com/news/the-fix/wp/2017/02/08/why-trumps-travel-ban-is-struggling-people-were-never-begging-for-it-in-the-first-place/

Brown, H., Guskin, E., & Mitchell, A. (2012). The role of social media in the arab uprisings. Retrieved from http://www.journalism.org/2012/11/28/role-social-media-arab-uprisings/

Cillizza, C. (2015). Millennials don't trust anyone. that's a big deal. Washington Post. Retrieved from https://www.washingtonpost.com/news/the-fix/wp/2015/04/30/millennials-dont-trust-anyone-what-else-is-new/

Crockett, Z. (2016). Millennials have very little confidence in most major institutions. Retrieved from https://www.vox.com/2016/9/28/13062286/millennials-confidence-in-government

Decker, L., Fromm, J., & Lindell, C. American millennials: Deciphering the enigma generation. Barkley.

Fromm, J. (2016). New study finds social media shapes millennial political involvement and engagement. Retrieved from http://www.forbes.com/sites/jefffromm/2016/06/22/new-study-finds-social-media-shapes-millennial-political-involvement-and-engagement/

Gallup. Confidence in institutions. Retrieved from http://www.gallup.com/poll/1597/Confidence-Institutions.aspx

Grabar, H. (2017). The uber boycott and lyft's ACLU donation herald a new era of corporate politics. Slate, Retrieved from http://www.slate.com/blogs/moneybox/2017/01/30/the_uber_boycott_and_lyft_s_aclu_donation_herald_a_new_era_of_corporate.html

Hawkins, A. J. (2017). Lyft surpasses uber in app downloads for the first time ever. Retrieved from https://www.theverge.com/2017/1/30/14443560/lyft-surpass-uber-app-downloads-deleteuber

Lopez, G. (2017). Why people are deleting uber from their phones after trump's executive order. Retrieved from https://www.vox.com/policy-and-politics/2017/1/29/14431246/uber-trump-muslim-ban

Nickalls, S. (2017). Here's how many people deleted their uber accounts. Retrieved from http://www.esquire.com/news-politics/news/a52806/deleted-uber-accounts/

Nieuwenkamp, R. (2015). Can companies really do well by doing good? the business case for corporate responsibility. Retrieved from http://oecdinsights.org/2015/11/02/can-companies-really-do-well-by-doing-good-the-business-case-for-corporate-responsibility/

Nieuwenkamp, R. (2016). 2016: CSR is dead! what's next? Retrieved from http://oecdinsights.org/2016/01/22/2016-csr-is-dead-whats-next/

Political polarization in the american public. (2014). Retrieved from http://www.people-press.org/2014/06/12/political-polarization-in-the-american-public/

Public Opinion Strategies, & GBA Strategies. (2016). The millennial economy. Ernst & Young, Economic Innovation Group. Retrieved from http://eig.org/millennial

Rapoza, K. (2013). Transparency international spells it out: Politicians are the most corrupt. Retrieved from http://www.forbes.com/sites/kenrapoza/2013/07/09/transparency-international-spells-it-out-politicians-are-the-most-corrupt/

Sanchez, R. (2016). Occupy wall street: 5 years later. Retrieved from http://www.cnn.com/2016/09/16/us/occupy-wall-street-protest-movements/index.html

The Center for Generational Kinetics. (2016). Infographic: Gen Z voter and political views election 2016. Retrieved from http://genhq.com/igen-gen-z-stance-on-politics-infographic/

Use of social networking technology | the institute of politics at harvard university. Retrieved from http://iop.harvard.edu/use-social-networking-technology

WETA. (2016). When power corrupts: 16 of the biggest political scandals of the last 50 years | washington week. Retrieved from http://www.pbs.org/weta/washingtonweek/blog-post/when-power-corrupts-16-biggest-political-scandals-last-50-years

When it comes to politics, do millennials care about anything? Retrieved from http://www.theatlantic.com/sponsored/allstate/when-it-comes-to-politics-do-millennials-care-about-anything/255/

Wines, M. (2017). It only seems that political corruption is rampant. The New York Times Retrieved from https://www.nytimes.com/2014/01/26/us/politics/it-only-seems-that-political-corruption-is-rampant.html

Worland, J. (2016). What to know about the dakota access pipeline protests. Retrieved from http://time.com/4548566/dakota-access-pipeline-standing-rock-sioux/

Sentiment References

Arnold, C. (2015). Economists say millennials should consider careers in trades. Retrieved from http://www.npr.org/2015/02/02/383335110/economists-say-millennials-should-consider-careers-in-trades

Bagley, R. O. (2013). The key to growth: Transformational change. Retrieved from http://www.forbes.com/sites/rebeccabagley/2013/01/02/the-key-to-growth-transformational-change/

Basu, T. (2015). Millennials don't like to call themselves millennials. Retrieved from http://time.com/4021479/millennial-generation-pew/

Cillizza, C. (2015). Millennials don't trust anyone. that's a big deal. Washington Post. Retrieved from https://www.washingtonpost.com/news/the-fix/wp/2015/04/30/millennials-dont-trust-anyone-what-else-is-new/

Collaborating in the cloud: Why it is important, and what to look for when evaluating a cloud-based collaboration solution. (2012). Cisco Systems.

The deloitte millennial survey 2017 - apprehensive millennials: Seeking stability and opportunities in an uncertain world. (2017). Deloitte.

Dogen, S. No wonder why millennials don't give A damn about money | financial samurai. Retrieved from http://www.financialsamurai.com/no-wonder-why-millennials-dont-give-a-damn-about-money/

EU referendum: The result in maps and charts. (2016). BBC News. Retrieved from http://www.bbc.com/news/uk-politics-36616028

Finances, social trends and technology (2014). Pew Research Center. Retrieved from http://www.pewsocialtrends.org/2014/03/07/chapter-3-finances-social-trends-and-technology/

Fleming, J. H. (2016). Americans' big debt burden growing, not evenly distributed Gallup. Retrieved from http://www.gallup.com/businessjournal/188984/americans-big-debt-burden-growing-not-evenly-distributed.aspx

Forbes Corporate Communications. (2013). Forbes insights survey reveals cloud collaboration increases business productivity and advances global communication. Retrieved from http://www.forbes.com/sites/forbespr/2013/05/20/forbes-insights-survey-reveals-cloud-collaboration-increases-business-productivity-and-advances-global-communication/

Fry, R. (2014). Young adults, student debt and economic well-being. Retrieved from http://www.pewsocialtrends.org/2014/05/14/young-adults-student-debt-and-economic-well-being/

Fry, R., & Caumont, A. (2014). 5 key findings about student debt. Retrieved from http://www.pewresearch.org/fact-tank/2014/05/14/5-key-findings-about-student-debt/

Gallup.Confidence in institutions. Retrieved from http://www.gallup.com/poll/1597/Confidence-Institutions.aspx

Gillenwater, R. (2015). Why millennials in the workplace 'don't care,' and 4 things you can do. Retrieved from https://www.entrepreneur.com/article/246437

Hakala, K. (2015). 13 lies we need to stop telling women about marriage. Retrieved from https://mic.com/articles/116458/13-lies-we-need-to-stop-telling-women-about-marriage

How we voted — by age, education, race and sexual orientation. (2016). Retrieved from http://college.usatoday.com/2016/11/09/how-we-voted-by-age-education-race-and-sexual-orientation/

Ipsos MORI. (2016). How britain voted in 2015. Retrieved from https://www.ipsos.com/ipsos-mori/en-uk/how-britain-voted-2015

Maynes, M. (2016). FullContact. Retrieved from https://www.fullcontact.com/blog/data-corruption-and-why-millennials-dont-care-about-your-company/

Millennials infographic. Retrieved from
http://www.goldmansachs.com/our-thinking/pages/millennials/

Mosendz, P. (2017). What this election taught us about millennial voters. Bloomberg. Retrieved from https://www.bloomberg.com/news/articles/2016-11-09/what-this-election-taught-us-about-millennial-voters

Patel Nadeya. (2016). Millennials don't care about the past. Retrieved from https://www.theodysseyonline.com/millennials-dont-care-about-the-past

Runciman, W. G. (1969). What is structuralism? The British Journal of Sociology, 20(3), 253-265. doi:10.2307/588951

Schulte, B. (2015). Millennials want a work-life balance. their bosses just don't get why. Washington Post. Retrieved from https://www.washingtonpost.com/local/millennials-want-a-work-life-balance-their-bosses-just-dont-get-why/2015/05/05/1859369e-f376-11e4-84a6-6d7c67c50db0_story.html

The Center for Information and Research on Civic Learning and Engagement. (2016). An estimated 24 million young people voted in 2016 election. Retrieved from http://civicyouth.org/an-estimated-24-million-young-people-vote-in-2016-election/

Tuition and fees and room and board over time. (2017). The College Board.

When it comes to politics, do millennials care about anything? Retrieved from http://www.theatlantic.com/sponsored/allstate/when-it-comes-to-politics-do-millennials-care-about-anything/255/

Young v old votes for bernie and hillary in the 2016 primaries. (2016). Retrieved from http://www.economist.com/blogs/graphicdetail/2016/04/daily-chart-19

Values References

Alper, B. A. (2015). Millennials are less religious than older americans, but just as spiritual. Retrieved from http://www.pewresearch.org/fact-tank/2015/11/23/millennials-are-less-religious-than-older-americans-but-just-as-spiritual/

Bradberry, T. (2016). Why every employee should have unlimited vacation days. Retrieved from http://www.forbes.com/sites/travisbradberry/2016/05/24/why-every-employee-should-have-unlimited-vacation-days/

Changing attitudes on gay marriage. (2016). Pew Research Center. Retrieved from http://www.pewforum.org/2016/05/12/changing-attitudes-on-gay-marriage/

Cohn, D., & Taylor, P. (2010). Baby boomers approach 65 – glumly. Retrieved from http://www.pewsocialtrends.org/2010/12/20/baby-boomers-approach-65-glumly/

David Binder Research. (2016). DBR airbnb survey summary AirBNB.

Desilver, D. (2014). The politics of american generations: How age affects attitudes and voting behavior. Retrieved from http://www.pewresearch.org/fact-tank/2014/07/09/the-politics-of-american-generations-how-age-affects-attitudes-and-voting-behavior/

Fingerhut, H. (2016). Millennials' views of news media, religious organizations grow more negative. Retrieved from http://www.pewresearch.org/fact-tank/2016/01/04/millennials-views-of-news-media-religious-organizations-grow-more-negative/

Frey, W. H. (2016). Diversity defines the millennial generation. Brookings. Retrieved from https://www.brookings.edu/blog/the-avenue/2016/06/28/diversity-defines-the-millennial-generation/

Fry, R. (2016). For first time in modern era, living with parents edges out other living arrangements for 18- to 34-year-olds. Retrieved from http://www.pewsocialtrends.org/2016/05/24/for-first-time-in-modern-era-living-with-parents-edges-out-other-living-arrangements-for-18-to-34-year-olds/

Fry, R., & Patten, E. (2015). How millennials today compare with their grandparents 50 years ago. Retrieved from http://www.pewresearch.org/fact-tank/2015/03/19/how-millennials-compare-with-their-grandparents/

Growing up LGBT in america. Human Rights Campaign.

Jones, J. M. (2015). U.S. baby boomers more likely to identify as conservative. Gallup Poll News Service. Retrieved from http://www.gallup.com/poll/181325/baby-boomers-likely-identify-conservative.aspx

Lewis, A. (2010). Looking behind the catholic sex abuse scandal. BBC News. Retrieved from http://news.bbc.co.uk/2/hi/8654789.stm

Livingston, G. (2015). Family size among mothers. Retrieved from http://www.pewsocialtrends.org/2015/05/07/family-size-among-mothers/

Masci, D. (2016). Q&A: Why millennials are less religious than older americans. Retrieved from http://www.pewresearch.org/fact-tank/2016/01/08/qa-why-millennials-are-less-religious-than-older-americans/

Millennials infographic. Retrieved from http://www.goldmansachs.com/our-thinking/pages/millennials/

Millennials prefer "Shopping down the street". (2016). The G Brief. Retrieved from http://thegbrief.com/articles/millennials-prefer-shopping-down-the-street-568

Rampell, C. (2016). Millennials aren't buying homes. good for them. The Washington Post. Retrieved from https://www.washingtonpost.com/opinions/millennials-arent-buying-homes--good-for-them/2016/08/22/818793be-68a4-11e6-ba32-5a4bf5aad4fa_story.html?utm_term=.cb71277c0dcc

St. Clair, B. (2016). The real reason so many millennials are living at home. Washington Post. Retrieved from https://www.washingtonpost.com/news/wonk/wp/2016/06/30/the-real-reason-so-many-millennials-are-living-at-home/

A survey of LGBT americans. (2013). Pew Research Center. Retrieved from http://www.pewsocialtrends.org/2013/06/13/a-survey-of-lgbt-americans/

Taylor, M. C. (2014). Fast, cheap and out of control: How hyper-consumerism drives us mad. Retrieved from http://www.salon.com/2014/11/02/fast_cheap_and_out_of_control_how_hyper_consumerism_drives_us_mad/

Thompson, D. (2016). The liberal millennial revolution. The Atlantic. Retrieved from https://www.theatlantic.com/politics/archive/2016/02/the-liberal-millennial-revolution/470826/

Wilkins, D. (2016). Why millennials love the sharing economy. SPOT. Retrieved from http://www.parkeasier.com/why-millennials-love-the-sharing-economy/

Engagement References

2014 global workforce study. (2014). Towers Watson.

Adkins, A. (2016). Brands aren't winning millennial consumers. Retrieved from http://www.gallup.com/businessjournal/192710/brands-aren-winning-millennial-consumers.aspx

Adkins, A. (2016). Millennials: The job-hopping generation. Retrieved from http://www.gallup.com/businessjournal/191459/millennials-job-hopping-generation.aspx

Adkins, A. (2016). What millennials want from work and life. Retrieved from http://www.gallup.com/businessjournal/191435/millennials-work-life.aspx

Brack, J., & Kelly, K. (2012). Maximizing millennials in the workplace. Retrieved from https://www.kenan-flagler.unc.edu/executive-development/custom-programs/~/media/DF1C11C056874DDA8097271A1ED48662.ashx

Burton, N. (2015). Empathy vs sympathy. Retrieved from https://www.psychologytoday.com/blog/hide-and-seek/201505/empathy-vs-sympathy

The deloitte millennial survey 2017 - apprehensive millennials: Seeking stability and opportunities in an uncertain world. (2017). Deloitte.

Discretionary effort. Retrieved from http://aubreydaniels.com/discretionary-effort

Donnelly, C., & Scaff, R. Who are the millennial shoppers? and what do they really want? Retrieved from https://www.accenture.com/us-en/insight-outlook-who-are-millennial-shoppers-what-do-they-really-want-retail

Hockenson, L. (2013). Engagement: The big word that means very little. Retrieved from http://mashable.com/2013/05/01/engagement-buzzword/

How millennials want to work and live; (2016). Gallup.

Kruse, K. (2012). What is employee engagement. Retrieved from http://www.forbes.com/sites/kevinkruse/2012/06/22/employee-engagement-what-and-why/

Millennials infographic. Retrieved from http://www.goldmansachs.com/our-thinking/pages/millennials/

Millennials: The new age of brand loyalty. (2014). Adroit Digital.

Nelson, B., & Rigoni, B. (2016). Few millennials are engaged at work. Retrieved from http://www.gallup.com/businessjournal/195209/few-millennials-engaged-work.aspx

Petro, G. (2013). Millennial engagement and loyalty -- make them part of the process. Retrieved from http://www.forbes.com/sites/gregpetro/2013/03/21/millennial-engagement-and-loyalty-make-them-part-of-the-process/

Way to work survey. (2015). Adecco Staffing. Retrieved from http://blog.adeccousa.com/way-to-work-survey-1/

ENDNOTES

About TAPO Institute

The TAPO Institute is a strategic think tank and advising consultancy focused on providing long-term solutions for workforce engagement and inclusion strategy. It draws its inspiration from today's generations being transparent, authentic, persistent and optimistic about inclusion.

About TAPO's Founder

Todd Corley is the Chief Diversity & Inclusion Officer at OhioHealth, one of FORTUNE magazine's "100 Best Companies to Work For". There, he leads efforts to embrace diversity within the organization, support OhioHealth's diverse patient population and work closely with senior leadership to coordinate OhioHealth's diversity and inclusion efforts as an integral part of the organizational vision. Corley comes to OhioHealth with nearly 20 years of diversity and inclusion leadership experience, most recently as founder and chief strategist at The TAPO Institute. He has received numerous awards and accolades that underscore his character and personal mission; among them: the 2016 recipient of Columbus Business First's "Lifetime Achievement Award" and the 2013 recipient of the inaugural "Claes Nobel World Betterment Award" by Mr. Claes Nobel (of the established Nobel Prize). Corley is also the author of

Fitch Path: A Cautionary Tale About A Moose, Millennials, Leadership & Transparency; which "offers an inspiring, expansive view of diversity" (Kirkus Reviews) and contributor of *The Great Global Check Out: Millennials, iGens, and the Epidemic of Disengagement.*